Estimates of the Impact of Restrictions on Cross-Border Trade in Services

Estimates of the Impact of Restrictions on Cross-Border Trade in Services

David Riker [1]

U.S. International Trade Commission, Office of Economics, Research Division

August 26, 2014

Abstract

I estimate the effect of import restrictions on cross-border trade in services using a sector-level gravity model. Then I use the model to simulate the expansion in U.S. services exports that would result from completely eliminating these restrictions in several major U.S. trade partners.

Keywords: trade in services, STRI, gravity model

JEL Codes: F13, F14

1. Introduction

In this paper, I estimate the effect of import restrictions on international trade in services using a sector-level gravity model.[2] The econometric model utilizes sector- and country-level data on trade, production, and expenditures from the World Input-Output Database (WIOD) and the Services Trade Restrictions Index (STRI) published by the World Bank. I use the econometric model to simulate the expansion in U.S. services exports that would result from completely eliminating import restrictions in several major U.S. trade partners.

The model is similar to the gravity model of trade in services in van der Marel and Shepherd (2013). Their study uses data for 2005 services trade flows from Francois et al. (2009) and a sector-level gravity model of trade to estimate the effects of trade restrictions (measured by

---

[1] This research note is the result of ongoing professional research of ITC Staff and is solely meant to represent the opinions and professional research of the author. It is not meant to represent in any way the views of the U.S. International Trade Commission or any of its individual Commissioners. I would like to thank Martha Lawless for many helpful comments on an earlier draft. Please address any correspondence to David.Riker@usitc.gov.

[2] According to WTO definitions, mode 1 includes cross-border services trade. Mode 3, the sale of services by foreign affiliates, is generally larger than mode 1 trade. For example, of the U.S. services provided to foreign markets in 2011, $606.0 billion were cross-border trade (mode 1), while $1,287 billion were sales through foreign affiliates (mode 3).

the World Bank's STRI). Their gravity model controls for multilateral resistance terms using importer and exporter country fixed effects.[3] They also control for the distance between the countries, whether they share a common language, and whether they have colonial ties. Van der Marel and Shepherd conclude that there is a significant link between the STRI measure of trade restrictions and lower volumes of trade in services, though the strength of the link varies by service sector. They find significant negative effects of the restrictions on cross-border trade in financial and transportation services.

This paper addresses the same set of issues – but with a different dataset and several variations on the methodology in van der Marel and Shepherd (2013). First, I use more recent data on trade in services. Second, my model includes sector-level measures of expenditures and production, rather than economy-wide GDP measures. Third, I use an econometric specification with linearized multilateral resistance terms, following Baier and Bergstrand (2009), rather than country fixed effects. Fourth, my model only includes the STRI for the importer country, while van der Marel and Shepherd (2013) includes a dyadic measure that interacts the STRI for the exporter country with the STRI for the importer country.[4]

The rest of this paper is organized into five sections. Section 2 describes the data that I use in the econometric analysis, and Section 3 describes the econometric specification. Section 4 reports the estimated parameters of the model, and Section 5 reports simulations based on the model. Section 6 concludes with ideas for further development of this line of research.

2. Data

The econometric model utilizes 2011 WIOD data on sector-level production and expenditures for each country, as well as sector-level bilateral trade in services.[5] Timmer et al. (2012) provides a detailed description of the construction of the WIOD data. The model also utilizes data on sector-level trade restrictions from the World Bank's Services Trade Restrictions

---

[3] This is one of the methods of estimating multilateral resistance terms in Anderson and van Wincoop (2003, 2004).

[4] The World Bank's STRI documentation indicates that a country's STRI measures the restrictions on its imports of services, not the restrictions on its exports.

[5] Recent examples of economic studies that utilize WIOD data include Costinot and Rodríguez -Clare (2014) and Timmer et al. (2014).

database. The STRI tries to isolate restrictions that affect a country's imports of services. The STRI values for each sector and country range from 0 (open without restrictions) to 100 (completely closed). The data cover five service sectors: financial, professional services (specifically accounting and legal), retail distribution, telecommunications, and transportation. The index values for OECD countries were constructed from public data, and the index values for non-OECD countries were constructed from responses to World Bank questionnaires.[6]

Table 1 reports values of the STRI for the United States and for several major U.S. trade partners for financial, telecommunications, and transportation services. I focus on these three service sectors because there is a close concordance between the WIOD and STRI databases. According to the STRI data, China and India are significantly more restrictive than the United States in all three sectors. Germany and United Kingdom are less restrictive than the United States in financial and telecommunications services but more restrictive in transportation services. Japan is less restrictive in financial services but more restrictive in telecommunications and transportation services.

3. Baier-Bergstrand Gravity Model at the Sector Level

The econometric model is based on the method for estimating gravity models in Baier and Bergstrand (2009). Their specification linearizes the multilateral resistance terms in the gravity model, so it is not necessary to control from them with country fixed effects or to estimate the multilateral resistance terms with non-linear methods.[7] Equations (1) through (3) summarize the econometric specification.[8]

$$x_{sod} - e_{sd} - y_{so} = \alpha_s + \beta(T_{sd} - MR\,T_{sd}) + \gamma(z_{od} - MR\,z_{od}) + \varepsilon_{sod} \tag{1}$$

$$MR\,T_{sod} = \sum_{j \neq d} \psi_{sj} T_{sd} + \sum_{k \neq o} \theta_{sk} T_{sk} - \sum_k \sum_{j \neq k} \psi_{sj} \theta_{sk} T_{sk} \tag{2}$$

$$MR\,z_{od} = \sum_{j \neq d} \psi_{sj} z_{jd} + \sum_{k \neq o} \theta_{sk} z_{ok} - \sum_k \sum_{j \neq k} \psi_{sj} \theta_{sk} z_{jk} \tag{3}$$

---

[6] Borchert, Gootiiz, and Mattoo (2012a,b) provide detailed descriptions of the World Bank's STRI.

[7] Head and Mayer (2014) discusses both of these approaches to multilateral resistance terms, as well as the method in Baier and Bergstrand (2009).

[8] Most gravity models include the expenditure and production terms on the right-hand side of the gravity equation and restrict the elasticity to be equal to one. However, this is equivalent to moving the expenditure and production terms to the left-hand side, as in equation (1).

The variable x_{sod} is the log of sector s exports from country of origin o to destination country d, e_{sd} is the log of country d expenditures on sector s services, y_{so} is the log of country o production of sector s services, T_{sd} is the STRI measure for sector s in country d, z_{od} represents a set of other explanatory variables that affect international trade costs, ψ_{sj} is the share of country j in global production of sector s services, θ_{sk} is the share of country k in global expenditures on sector s services, and ε_{sod} is the error term of the model.[9]

The log-linear specification in equations (1) through (3) is well-suited for the comparative static simulations in Section 5, because it provides an estimate of the trade impact of T_{sd} that includes its impact on the multilateral resistance terms.[10] The model uses sector-specific measures of expenditure and production, as recommended in Anderson (2011), rather than broad measures of economic size like GDP.

I impute STRI values for countries that are not covered in the World Bank's database, because the multilateral resistance term in equation (2) requires a value of T_{sd} for every country. Using data for the countries included in the STRI database, I regress their STRI on their level of economic development (measured by the log of GDP per capita), separately for each of the service sectors. I use these simple functions to impute STRI values for the countries not included in the STRI database.

4. Econometric Estimates

Next, I estimate the parameters of equation (1) using a cross-section of sector-level trade, production, and expenditure values from the world input-output table for 2011. I consider several versions of the econometric specification, with different sets of explanatory variables. I use a Poisson estimator, following van der Marel and Shepherd (2013).[11] The model pools across the three service sectors.

I find that the STRI of the importing country and the distance between the pair had significant negative effects on cross-border trade in services, and that common language had a

---

[9] The variable j is an index of the countries of origin, and the variable k is an index of destination countries.

[10] Specifically, it quantifies what Head and Mayer (2014) calls the "modular trade impact" or MTI. The MTI holds expenditure and production levels fixed.

[11] Santos Silva and Tenreyro (2006, 2011) show that the Poisson model is preferable to Ordinary Least Squares for estimating log-linear models when there are zeroes and heteroskedasticity in the data.

significant positive effect. Table 2 reports the coefficient estimates. All of the versions of the model include sector fixed effects and the log of the distance between the pair of countries. Two of the versions of the model include variables that indicate whether the countries share a common language or have colonial ties. The estimated coefficients on the STRI, distance, and common language terms are similar in magnitude across the models. The third model also includes a colonial ties term as an additional explanatory variable. The estimated coefficient on the colonial ties term is negative, but it is not significantly different from zero. The inclusion of the colonial ties term has little effect on the estimated coefficient on STRI, which is the focus of this paper. The Akaike Information Criterion (AIC) at the bottom of Table 2 is a measure of goodness of fit that takes into account the differences in degrees of freedom. Model 1 has the lowest AIC and is therefore the preferred model among the three.

The estimates in Table 2 are qualitatively similar to the estimates in van der Marel and Shepherd (2013): they have the same sign on the trade restrictions, international distance and common language. The magnitudes of the coefficient estimates are not really comparable, since van der Marel and Shepherd (2013) use a very different function form for the STRI term.[12]

5. Simulated Effects of Trade Liberalization

This section goes a step beyond van der Marel and Shepherd (2013) by applying the coefficients for Version A of the model in a series of counterfactual simulations. The simulations estimate the effect on U.S. services exports if the trade partner were to completely eliminate restrictions on its imports from all countries.[13] These trade impact calculations incorporate additional information: they are based not only on the estimated coefficients of the econometric model but also on the country's baseline STRI value and the volume of its services imports prior the elimination of the import restrictions.

It is important to keep in mind that the model and the simulation only quantify the impact on cross-border trade in services (mode 1). Reductions in services trade restrictions could also

---

[12] They interact the STRI value for the importing country with the STRI value for the exporting country, as noted above.

[13] Specifically, I simulate the trade impact of reducing the value of T_{sd} from its current value to zero.

have a significant effect on sales through foreign affiliates (mode 3), but these effects are not included in the simulated effects.[14]

Table 3 reports the value of U.S. exports in financial services in 2011 and the simulated increase in U.S. exports in this sector if the trade partner were to completely eliminate its restrictions on imports of financial services. Each row represents a different importing country. The table reports point estimates and 95% confidence intervals for the simulated increases in exports, in millions of U.S. dollars and in percent changes. The confidence intervals indicate that the trade impacts are all significantly greater than zero, though the intervals are fairly wide in some cases. China and India have the largest simulated increases in U.S. exports of financial services, both in dollar values ($186.0 million and $42.2 million) and in percent changes (10.14 percent and 3.76 percent). Germany has the smallest simulated increase ($7.7 million or 0.23 percent). In the financial services sector, Germany is a relatively large export market of the United States, second to the United Kingdom, but it has the smallest trade impact because its STRI is already very low.

Table 4 reports the same simulation for U.S. exports of telecommunications. In this case, China and Japan have the largest simulated increases in U.S. exports, both in dollar values ($233.3 million and $34.2 million) and in percent changes (23.00 percent and 7.16 percent). Germany and the United Kingdom have no simulated increases, because their STRIs in telecommunications are already zero (open without restrictions). The simulated increase in exports to India is small, even though India's STRI in telecommunications is relatively high (table 1).

Finally, Table 5 reports simulations for U.S. exports of transportation services. China and Germany have the largest simulated increases in U.S. exports when measured in dollar values ($918.6 million and $437.3 million). The effect on imports into India is greater than the effect on imports into China or Germany when measured in percent changes (an 11.95 percent increase in imports into India, compared to an 8.73 percent increase in imports into China and a 4.97 percent increase in imports into Germany).

---

[14] Barattieri et al. (2014) examines the empirical relationship between the STRI and model 3 transactions. The authors model the effects of the restrictions on cross-border mergers and acquisitions in services sectors.

6. Conclusions

I conclude with several ideas for further development of this line of research. The first idea is to try to find additional variables that contribute to international trade costs, hopefully at the sector level. The second is to develop alternative methods for imputing STRI values for the countries that are not included in the World Bank's database. The third is to extend the analysis to the mode 3 supply of services to foreign markets. The fourth is to estimate general equilibrium trade impacts that also take into account the effects on sector-level expenditures and production, rather than the modular trade impacts that are simulated in Section 5. The fifth is to estimate the effects of eliminating the trade restrictions on aggregate economic welfare in the United States and the importing country using the methodology in Costinot and Rodríguez-Clare (2014).

References

Anderson, J. and E. van Wincoop (2003): "Gravity with Gravitas: A Solution to the Border Puzzle." *American Economic Review* 93 (1): 170-192.

Anderson, J. and E. van Wincoop (2004): "Trade Costs." *Journal of Economic Literature* 42 (3): 691-751.

Anderson, J. (2010): "The Gravity Model." *Annual Review of Economics*, Vol. 3: 133-160.

Baier, S. L. and J. H. Bergstrand (2009): "Bonus Vetas OLS: A Simple Method for Approximating International Trade-Cost Effects Using the Gravity Equation." *Journal of International Economics* 77 (1): 77-85.

Barattieri, A., I. Borchert and A. Mattoo (2014): "Cross-Border Mergers and Acquisitions in Services." World Bank Policy Research Working Paper 6905.

Borchert, I., B. Gootiiz and A. Mattoo (2012a): "Guide to the Services Trade Restrictions Database." World Bank Policy Research Working Paper 6108.

Borchert, I., B. Gootiiz and A. Mattoo (2012b): "Policy Barriers to International Trade in Services: Evidence from a New Database." World Bank Policy Research Working Paper 6109.

Costinot, A. and A. Rodríguez-Clare (2014): "Trade Theory with Numbers: Quantifying the Consequences of Globalization" in G. Gopinath, E. Helpman, and K.Rogoff, eds., *Handbook of International Economics, Volume 4*. Elsevier.

Francois, J., O. Pinduyk, and J. Woerz (2009): "Trends in International Trade and FDI in Services." Discussion Paper No. 200908-02 (Rotterdam: Institute for International and Development Economics).

Head, K. and T. Meyer (2014): "Gravity Equations: Workhorse, Toolkit, and Cookbook," in G. Gopinath, E. Helpman, and K.Rogoff, eds., *Handbook of International Economics, Volume 4.* Elsevier.

Santos Silva and Tenreyro (2006): "The Log of Gravity." *Review of Economics and Statistics* 88 (4): 641-658.

Santos Silva and Tenreyro (2011): "Further Simulation Evidence on the Performance of the Poisson-PML Estimator." *Economics Letters* 112 (2): 220-222.

Timmer, M. ed. (2012): "The World Input-Output Database (WIOD): Contents, Sources, and Methods." WIOD Working Paper No. 10.

Timmer, M., A. Erumban, B. Los, R. Stehrer, and G. de Vries (2014): "Slicing Up Global Value Chains." *Journal of Economic Perspectives* 28 (2): 99-118.

van der Marel, E. and B. Shepherd (2013): "Services Trade, Regulation and Regional Integration: Evidence from Sectoral Data." *World Economy* 36(11): 1393-1405.

Table 1. Services Trade Restrictions Index (STRI) from the World Bank

	Financial	Telecommunications	Transportation
United States	21.4	0.0	7.9
China	34.8	50.0	19.3
Germany	1.3	0.0	24.4
India	48.1	50.0	62.4
Japan	1.9	25.0	15.6
United Kingdom	0.6	0.0	23.1

Source: Services Trade Restrictions Database at
http://iresearch.worldbank.org/servicetrade/aboutData.htm

Table 2. Econometric Estimates

Dependent Variable: Log of Bilateral Exports by Services Sector in 2011, minus the Log of Sector Expenditures in the Destination Country and the Log of Sector Production in the Source Country

Explanatory Variables	Version A	Version B	Version C
STRI with Multilateral Resistance Term	-0.0407 (0.0127)	-0.0378 (0.0129)	-0.0376 (0.0130)
Log of Distance with Multilateral Resistance Term	-1.1805 (0.0704)	-1.4773 (0.0640)	-1.4763 (0.0637)
Common Language with Multilateral Resistance Term		1.8303 (0.1877)	1.8396 (0.2010)
Colonial Ties with Multilateral Resistance Term			-0.1325 (0.4846)
Telecommunications Sector Indicator Variable	0.5620 (0.4105)	0.7197 (0.3896)	0.7209 (0.3904)
Transportation Sector Indicator Variable	-0.0423 (0.3929)	0.1819 (0.3758)	0.1836 (0.3756)
Constant	-16.0993 (0.3494)	-17.3294 (0.2561)	-17.3249 (0.2574)
Pseudo R^2 Statistic	0.2898	0.2997	0.2997
Akaike Information Criterion	10.25	12.25	14.25
Number of Observations	4,800	4,800	4,800

Note: Robust standard errors reported in parentheses.

Table 3. Simulations for the Financial Services Sector Based on Version A

Importing Country	U.S. Exports in 2011	Simulated Increase in U.S. Exports in the Financial Services Sector	
	in Millions of USD	in Millions of USD	Percent Change
China	1,834	186.0 (66.7 – 305.3)	10.14 (3.64 – 16.65)
Germany	3,277	7.7 (3.0 – 12.4)	0.23 (0.09 – 0.38)
India	1,122	42.2 (15.9 – 68.5)	3.76 (1.42 – 6.10)
Japan	4,074	20.0 (7.7 – 32.2)	0.49 (0.19 – 0.79)
United Kingdom	16,096	17.9 (7.0 – 28.9)	0.11 (0.04 – 0.18)

Note: The 95% confidence intervals for the simulated increases are reported in parentheses.

Table 4. Simulations for the Telecommunications Sector Based on Version A

Importing Country	U.S. Exports in 2011	Simulated Increase in U.S. Exports in the Telecommunications Sector	
	in Millions of USD	in Millions of USD	Percent Change
China	1,014	233.3 (75.4 – 391.1)	23.00 (7.44 – 38.57)
Germany	2,071	None: STRI Already Zero	None: STRI Already Zero
India	15	0.4 (0.2 – 0.7)	2.78 (1.06 – 4.50)
Japan	477	34.2 (12.6 – 55.8)	7.16 (2.63 – 11.69)
United Kingdom	2,371	None: STRI Already Zero	None: STRI Already Zero

Note: The 95% confidence intervals for the simulated increases are reported in parentheses.

Table 5. Simulations for the Transportation Services Sector Based on Version A

Importing Country	U.S. Exports in 2011	Simulated Increase in U.S. Exports in the Transportation Services Sector	
	in Millions of USD	in Millions of USD	Percent Change
China	10,522	918.6 (333.3 – 1,503.8)	8.73 (3.17 – 14.3)
Germany	8,799	437.3 (163.5 – 711.1)	4.97 (1.86 – 8.08)
India	587	70.2 (24.8 – 115.5)	11.95 (4.23 – 19.67)
Japan	5,450	231.2 (86.9 – 375.4)	4.24 (1.60 – 6.89)
United Kingdom	3,542	97.7 (37.2 – 158.3)	2.76 (1.05 – 4.47)

Note: The 95% confidence intervals for the simulated increases are reported in parentheses.